My H

Julie Haydon

MW01254049

Contents

Good Smells

This is my nose.

I smell things with my nose.

Some things smell good.

Some things smell bad.

Gran grows **herbs** in her garden. Some of the herbs smell good.

Gran's Herb Bags

Gran makes herb bags.

She cuts some herbs.

She puts them up to dry.

She puts the herbs

inside little bags.

Herb bags smell good.

I want a herb bag

for my room.

Gran will help me

to make a herb bag.

What I Need

To make my herb bag,
I need:

- cloth

- scissors

- stuffing

- a spoon

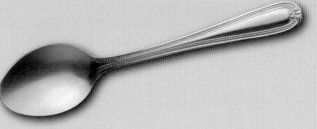

- dry herbs that smell good

- a rubber band

- ribbon

The Cloth

My cloth is blue
on the outside
and white on the inside.

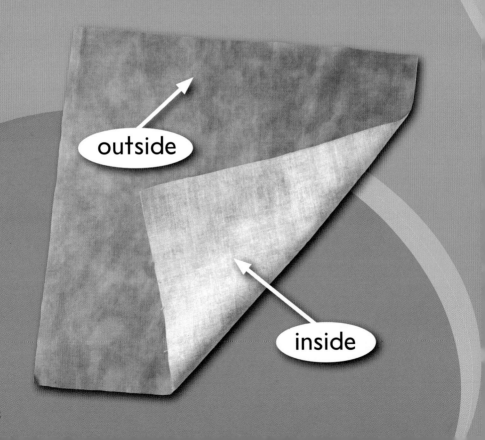

outside

inside

Gran helps me cut the cloth.

She cuts it into a square.

The Stuffing

I put the stuffing
on the inside of the cloth.
The stuffing will make
the bag round.
We will not see
the stuffing.

The Dry Herbs

I put some dry herbs
on a spoon.
The herbs smell good.
I put the herbs
on the stuffing.

My Herb Bag

I put the ends of the cloth over the herbs and stuffing. Gran helps me.

Gran puts a rubber band
around the cloth.
Then we put a ribbon
on the bag.

I put the herb bag
in my room.

I like my herb bag.

Now my room
will smell good!

Glossary

herbs